99 FAVORITE AMISH Recipes

GEORGIA VAROZZA

D0967860

HARVEST HOUSE PUBLISHERS
EUGENE, OREGON

Unless otherwise indicated, all Scripture quotations are from the Holy Bible, New International Version®, NIV®. Copyright © 1973, 1978, 1984, 2011 by Biblica, Inc.® Used by permission. All rights reserved worldwide.

Verses marked KJV are from the King James Version of the Bible.

Cover by Dugan Design Group, Bloomington, Minnesota

99 FAVORITE AMISH RECIPES

Copyright © 2015 Georgia Varozza
Published by Harvest House Publishers
Eugene, Oregon 97402
www.harvesthousepublishers.com

Library of Congress Cataloging-in-Publication Data
    Varozza, Georgia
    99 favorite Amish recipes / Georgia Varozza.
       pages cm
    Includes index.
    ISBN 978-0-7369-6250-6 (pbk.)
    ISBN 978-0-7369-6251-3 (eBook)
    1. Amish cooking. 2. Cooking—United States. I. Title. II. Title: Ninety-nine favorite Amish recipes.
    TX721.V277 2015
    641.5'66—dc23

                                   2014042866

Printed in China

    15 16 17 18 19 20 21 22 23 / RDS-JH / 10 9 8 7 6 5 4 3 2 1

To my family—
Who give me the very best reasons
(and counting!)
to keep moving forward.
It's worth saying again: I love you!

To Harvest House Publishers,
and most especially to Nick Harrison—
Who helped give me the courage to try.

To God—
Who looked at this daughter of His and said,
I will love you and guide you and protect you,
so get on with your life.
I've got you in the palm of My hand.

With these encouragers in my corner,
how can I go wrong?
I'm seriously blessed, and I thank you all.

CONTENTS

INTRODUCTION

I've written several books based on the Amish, and I never tire of thinking about their culture, their self-reliance, and most especially their food. Amish women prepare the kinds of meals I love to serve my family. Good, hearty fare, with plenty of the ingredients supplied from the backyard garden and farmyard during the warmer months and pantry shelves groaning with hundreds of home-canned jars of food come fall to see them through the cold winter months. The seasonal cycles are constant, and there's a certain quiet pride in knowing one's family will not go to bed hungry, no matter what the vagaries of inclement weather may be.

I think that's a large part of why I love to write cookbooks and blog about cooking and home life. I have this unfailing hope that young women will heed the call to care well for their loved ones and be confident and proud of their homemaking skills. I'm not talking about housekeeping—having everything just so, and the house so clean you could "eat off the floor" as my mom used to say. No, I truly do mean *homemaking*—the making of a home—that one place a family can return to each day and know they will be loved and encouraged and valued and, yes, fed.

My hope is that you'll try the recipes in this book. And if that endeavor spurs you on in your efforts to care for your family, then this little book will have been of good service. My prayer for all women—young or old, single or married, childless or bursting at the seams with little ones—is that, like the Amish, you will find great joy in your home life and "lead a quiet and peaceable life in all godliness and honesty" (1 Timothy 2:2 KJV).

May God's richest blessings be yours!

Georgia

BEST-EVER BREAKFASTS

Ah, breakfast. It's the most important meal of the day. Our bodies need that early-morning sustenance so we have the necessary energy to see us through the day. It seems to be a modern notion that we can haul ourselves out of bed at the last minute, rush around getting ready for the day, and then leave home without stopping long enough to eat a proper breakfast...and yet somehow manage to perform flawlessly.

Not so. Do yourself and your family a favor and sit down to a decent breakfast. You'll be so glad you did.

In this section you'll find lots to choose from. Some of the recipes can be started the night before and some are quick and easy, while others take a bit more time. And because the Amish love to eat pie and other sweets morning, noon, *and* night, you'll find a few quick pie recipes here as well. Making a pie crust does take some time, so if you want pie in a hurry, you can always buy store-bought pie shells and save that step. (And can you just imagine what your family will think when you bring pie to the breakfast table? Once they recover from their astonishment, they'll be happy to nominate you as Mom of the Year!)

Let's get started.

Because of the LORD's great love we are not
consumed, for his compassions never fail. They are
new every morning; great is your faithfulness.

<small>LAMENTATIONS 3:22-23</small>

Dear Lord, as I begin my day, help me to remember
that You are the potter and I am the clay. I pray that
today I will cheerfully submit to Your will for me
instead of charging ahead on my own. For Your ways
are perfect, and I am thankful that my life is in Your
hands. Help me to be a willing worker, doing good
to others and pointing them to You. Bless the work of
my hands, Lord, as I tend to the needs of my family,
and may Your Spirit dwell richly in us all. Amen.

1 Amish Apea Cake

4 cups flour
2 cups brown sugar
1 cup shortening, melted
1 tsp. baking soda
1 cup milk

In a large mixing bowl, combine all ingredients and stir to mix well. Pour batter into 3 8-inch pie pans. If desired, sprinkle cinnamon sugar on top.

Bake at 350° for 35-40 minutes.

It's good plain, or try it with some jam, maple syrup, or powdered sugar spooned over the top.

Notes:

2 Amish Apea Cake, Deluxe Version

2 cups flour
¾ cup brown sugar, packed
1½ tsp. baking powder
½ tsp. ground cinnamon
½ cup cold butter, cut into 12 pieces
⅓ cup raisins
⅓ cup chopped walnuts
1 egg
1 tsp. vanilla
½ cup milk

Grease a 9- or 10-inch pie plate. Preheat oven to 350°.

In a large mixing bowl, combine the flour, brown sugar, baking powder, and cinnamon. Stir with a large wooden spoon until well mixed. Cut in the butter, using a pastry cutter or two forks, until the mixture resembles coarse crumbs. Stir in the raisins and walnuts.

In a small bowl, beat the egg with a fork and then add the vanilla and milk and stir until well combined. Add to the flour mixture and stir with the wooden spoon until well mixed.

Spoon batter into the prepared pie plate and smooth the top of the batter. (You can sprinkle some cinnamon sugar over the top of the batter if desired.)

Bake for 30 minutes or until a toothpick inserted in the center comes out clean. Allow cake to cool for at least 15 minutes before cutting.

Notes:

3 Baked Oatmeal

This can be mixed together the night before.

1 cup oil
⅔ cup brown sugar or slightly more than ½ cup honey
6 cups rolled oats
3 tsp. baking powder
2 tsp. salt
2 cups milk
6 eggs

Mix together the oil, sugar or honey, and eggs. Add the oats, baking powder, salt, and milk; mix well.

Pour batter into a lightly buttered 13 x 9-inch baking pan and bake in a preheated 350° oven for 30 minutes.

Place warm baked oatmeal in a bowl and top with warm milk, cinnamon, and brown sugar.

Baked oatmeal is especially favored by children.

Notes:

4 Blueberry Muffins

⅓ cup butter
¾ cup sugar
1 egg, lightly beaten
1 cup milk
2 cups flour
4 tsp. baking powder
½ tsp. salt
1 cup blueberries, fresh or frozen

Cream together the butter and sugar. Add the egg and milk and mix. Mix together the flour, baking powder, and salt and add that to the egg mixture. Add blueberries last and gently mix the fruit into the batter.

Pour batter about ⅔ full into greased or paper-lined muffin tins. (You can sprinkle sugar or a combination of cinnamon and sugar on top of each muffin if desired.)

Bake at 375° for 20 minutes or until done.

I have made this recipe using a half-pint jar of my home-canned blueberries. I drain them well before adding them to the batter. (And I save the juice to drink later—it's so good iced or added to 7Up or ginger ale.)

Notes:

5 Bran Muffins

1 cup flour
3½ tsp. baking powder
½ tsp. salt
2 T. brown sugar
1 cup bran
1 egg, slightly beaten
⅓ cup milk
2 T. shortening, melted

In a large bowl, mix together the flour, baking powder, salt, and brown sugar; add the bran and mix again.

Combine the beaten egg, milk, and melted shortening; add to the dry ingredients and mix just until incorporated.

Pour batter into greased muffin tins and bake in a preheated 425° oven for 25 minutes or until done.

Notes:

6 Bread Omelet

½ loaf day-old bread, cut into cubes
½ cup butter
3 eggs, slightly beaten
½ cup milk
salt and pepper to taste

In a large fry pan, brown the bread cubes in the butter.

Mix together the eggs, milk, and salt and pepper to taste. Pour egg mixture over the bread cubes and fry until eggs are cooked through.

This is a perfect recipe for the frugal at heart!

Notes:

7 Buttermilk Biscuits

2 cups flour
½ tsp. salt
3 tsp. baking powder
½ tsp. baking soda
3 T. shortening
1 cup buttermilk

Sift together dry ingredients. Cut in shortening until mixture resembles coarse crumbles. Add buttermilk all at once. Mix with a fork until it forms a ball. Turn out the dough onto a floured surface and knead for 30 seconds. Roll out the dough to a ½-inch thickness and then cut with a biscuit cutter.

Place biscuits on an ungreased cookie sheet and bake at 425° for 15 minutes.

If you don't have buttermilk, you can use regular milk, but omit the baking soda and increase the baking powder to 4 teaspoons and the shortening to 5 tablespoons. Watch the biscuits as they bake because they may need a few extra minutes in the oven.

Notes:

8 Buttermilk Oatmeal Pancakes

Start the night before.

2 cups rolled oats
2 cups buttermilk, plus a bit more if needed
1 cup flour
2 tsp. sugar
1½ tsp. baking powder
1½ tsp. baking soda
1 tsp. salt
2 eggs
2 T. butter, melted and cooled slightly

In a mixing bowl, combine the oats and 2 cups buttermilk. Cover and refrigerate overnight.

In another mixing bowl, mix together the flour, sugar, baking powder, baking soda, and salt. Cover and set aside overnight.

The next morning, remove the oats and buttermilk mixture from the refrigerator and set aside.

In a large mixing bowl, whisk the eggs until they are light and frothy. Add the melted butter and mix together. Next, add the oatmeal/buttermilk mixture and mix well. Blend in the flour mixture; you will need to stir with a large wooden spoon at this point because the mixture will be very thick. If it appears too dry, you can add a few more tablespoons of buttermilk.

Fry the pancakes in a greased fry pan or griddle, turning once and cooking well on both sides. These pancakes really puff up, so it's better to cook them on a bit lower heat than usual but for a longer time.

Serve them hot from the griddle with butter and maple syrup.

These pancakes really fill a person up. They are hearty and so tasty that it's easy to eat "just one more"!

Notes:

9 Buttermilk Pie Crust

Makes 1 double, or 2 single crusts.

2½ cups flour
2 T. sugar
½-1 tsp. salt (use smaller amount if using salted butter;
    larger amount if butter is unsalted)
½ cup butter, cut into small pieces
½ cup shortening, chilled
¼ cup plus 2 T. cold buttermilk

In a large mixing bowl, combine flour, sugar, and salt. Add butter and shortening and mix until mixture resembles coarse crumbles. (Use a pastry blender, two forks or knives, or your hands—but if using your hands, work fast so the butter doesn't begin softening.)

Add buttermilk and mix with a fork until clumps form. Press together to form a ball. Divide in half and re-form dough into two smaller balls. Wrap each ball of dough in plastic wrap and refrigerate for 1 hour before rolling out and making crust. (If dough is tightly wrapped, it can stay fresh in your refrigerator for up to a week.)

Bake pie crust in preheated 425° oven for 12-15 minutes or until golden. (If baking crust empty, put a cup of raw white rice or small white beans into the bottom of the crust before baking. The weight of the rice or beans will keep the bottom of the crust from puffing up while baking. You can save the rice or beans to use for future pie crusts by cooling completely and then storing in an airtight, marked container.)

Notes:

10 Cinnamon Rolls

¾ cup milk
¾ cup water
½ cup shortening or lard
½ cup sugar
2 eggs
2 tsp. salt
4½ tsp. (2 pkg.) active dry yeast, dissolved in ½ cup lukewarm
    water
7 cups flour, more or less
½ cup butter, melted
cinnamon and sugar mixtures

Sugar Glaze (optional):
1½ cups powdered sugar
2-3 T. water

Heat milk and water together until scalded. Cool to lukewarm.

Mix together shortening, sugar, eggs, and salt. Add milk mixture and
stir well. Add dissolved yeast and stir well again. Add enough of the
flour so the dough pulls away from the sides of the bowl. Turn out
dough ball onto a floured surface and add the remaining flour as
needed to keep dough from sticking as you knead for 5 minutes.

Place dough in a large greased bowl, turning dough ball so entire surface is greased. Cover with a towel and let rise until double in bulk,
about 1 hour. Roll dough fairly thin so it's in a long rectangle shape.
Pour melted butter over the dough and sprinkle heavily with a cinnamon and sugar mixture. (You can also use brown sugar.) Roll up from
the long side, jelly-roll fashion, and then cut into rounds about 1-inch
thick. Place on greased baking sheets with their sides not quite touch-
ing and let rise about 45 minutes.

Notes:

Baked in preheated 350° oven for about 15-20 minutes or until done.

To make sugar glaze: Mix together the powdered sugar and water until well blended and of desired consistency. Drizzle over cooled cinnamon rolls.

11 Cornmeal Mush

3 cups cold water
1 cup cornmeal
1 tsp. salt

Mix together all ingredients and bring to a boil, stirring constantly. Cover and simmer on very low heat for 20 minutes. (If the heat is turned up too high the cornmeal will stick to the bottom of the pot and burn.)

You can serve it up into bowls at this point and eat it like a porridge or put it in a loaf pan and set in the refrigerator until chilled. Then cut it in slices and fry in bacon drippings or oil until golden on each side.

Cornmeal Mush tastes great with Tomato Gravy (page 37) spooned over the top. Or you can add some cooked chopped bacon to the batter before frying for a special treat.

Notes:

12 Crumb Pie

2 cups flour
1 heaping cup brown sugar
1 tsp. baking soda
1½ T. shortening
½ cup buttermilk or sour cream
small pinch salt
1 9-inch, unbaked pie shell

Preheat oven to 375°.

Mix together the flour, brown sugar, and baking soda. Cut in the shortening and blend well. Add the buttermilk or sour cream and rub mixture until coarse crumbs form. Place crumbs into the pie shell. Bake for 40 minutes or until done.

This is an old-time recipe with only a few ingredients. But it really hits the spot when you have a sweet tooth that needs attention!

13 Custard "Chess" Pie

4 eggs
½ cup sugar
¼ tsp. salt
1 tsp. vanilla
2½ cups scalded milk
1 9-inch, unbaked pie crust

Preheat oven to 475°.

In a large bowl, beat eggs; add sugar, salt, and vanilla and mix thoroughly. Slowly pour in the scalded milk while stirring, and then

Notes:

immediately pour custard into pie crust. Place pie in the oven and immediately reduce heat to 425°. Bake for 35 minutes, or until a knife inserted halfway between the center of pie and edge comes out clean.

Classic. I love to put sweetened whipped cream on top, but it's just as good plain and slightly warm.

14 Easy Apple Fritters

1 cup flour
1½ tsp. baking powder
2 T. sugar
½ tsp. salt
¾ cup milk
1 egg
4 large apples
shortening for frying

In a medium-sized bowl, mix together the flour, baking powder, sugar, and salt. Add the milk and egg and beat batter until smooth.

Peel and core apples and slice into rings about ¼-inch thick.

Melt shortening in a heavy-duty deep-sided skillet (cast iron works well); you want the melted shortening to be about ½-inch deep. Dip apple rings in batter and drop into the skillet. Fry until golden brown, turning once so both sides are cooked. Drain fritters on paper towels and then sprinkle liberally with cinnamon sugar.

Notes:

15 German Egg Pancakes

5 eggs, separated
½ cup milk
1 cup flour

In a large mixing bowl, beat the egg yolks until very light. Add the milk and flour gradually, mixing well after each addition. Mix until the batter is smooth.

In another large bowl, beat the egg whites until they are stiff. Fold the whites gently into the batter.

Drop by large spoonfuls on a hot greased griddle or fry pan, turning once. Serve hot, sprinkled with powdered sugar or spread with jam.

16 Graham "Nuts" Cereal

3½ cups whole wheat flour
1 cup brown sugar
1 tsp. salt
1 tsp. baking soda
1 tsp. ground cinnamon
2 cups buttermilk
2 tsp. vanilla

In a large bowl, combine all ingredients and mix well. Pour out onto an oiled 12 x 16-inch low-sided baking pan (jelly roll pans work well) and spread evenly with a spatula. Bake in a preheated 350° oven for 20 minutes or until the batter is firm and has begun to shrink away slightly from the sides of the pan. With a spatula, completely loosen the hot "cake" and allow to cool on a rack for several hours.

Notes:

Preheat oven to 275°. Break "cake" into chunks and pass them through a coarse-bladed meat grinder or push through a food screen or colander that has ¼-inch grids. Divide crumbs between two 12 x 16-inch baking pans.

Bake for 30 minutes, stirring every 10 minutes. Let cool completely and store in airtight containers.

Serve as a cold cereal with milk, or sprinkle on top of yogurt, ice cream, or when baking a fruit crisp, etc.

17 Granola

2 cups whole wheat flour
6 cups rolled oats
1 cup coconut
1 cup wheat germ
1 T. salt
½ cup water
1 cup oil
1 cup honey
2 tsp. vanilla

Combine dry ingredients in a large mixing bowl. Blend liquid ingredients and then add to the large bowl and mix thoroughly. Spread out on 2 greased cookie sheets or jelly roll pans and bake at 250° for 1 hour, stirring occasionally, or until dry and golden.

Store in an airtight container after completely cooled.

You can also add nuts, sunflower seeds, or raisins, if desired. Also, I often omit the wheat germ, increase the flour a wee bit, and call it good. We never seem to miss it.

Notes:

18 Ham and Tater Tot Casserole

1 package frozen Tater Tots or hash browns
8 oz. Velveeta cheese, cubed
6 eggs
¼ cup milk
salt and pepper to taste
½ cup cooked ham, cubed

Butter or grease a 9 x 9-inch baking dish and place the Tater Tots over the bottom. Next, add the Velveeta cheese.

Whisk together the eggs and milk and season with salt and pepper. Pour milk mixture over the Tater Tots and bake at 350° for 45 minutes. Remove from the oven and sprinkle the ham over the top; return to the oven for another 15 minutes or until eggs are completely set.

19 Hush Puppies

1 cup cornmeal
1 tsp. baking powder
½ tsp. salt
1 egg
½ cup milk (may need a bit more)
4 slices bacon (optional)

If using bacon, cut up and fry the bacon. (Save the grease for frying the hush puppies.)

In a large bowl, mix together the dry ingredients.

In another bowl, mix together the egg and milk and then add it to the dry ingredients; mix well. Add bacon if using and mix well again.

Notes:

Drop by large spoonfuls into bacon grease or oil and fry until golden brown.

Serve with maple syrup or eat plain.

20 Layered Breakfast Baked Casserole

12 slices bread
1 lb. thinly sliced ham, divided
2 cups shredded cheddar cheese, divided
6 large eggs
3 cups milk
1 tsp. dry mustard powder
1 tsp. onion powder
½ tsp. salt
½ tsp. pepper
¼ cup butter, melted
2 cups cornflakes, crushed

Grease a 9 x 13-inch baking dish and preheat oven to 350°.

Line the greased baking dish with 6 slices of bread. Layer half of the ham over the bread and sprinkle with half of the cheese. Repeat these layers one more time.

In a large mixing bowl, combine eggs, milk, dry mustard, onion powder, salt, and pepper and mix well. Slowly pour the egg mixture over the bread layers in the baking dish.

Mix the melted butter with the cornflakes and sprinkle evenly over the top of the casserole.

Bake 45-50 minutes or until set.

Notes:

21 Mama's Pie Crust

For Single Crust:
1½ cups sifted flour
½ tsp. salt
½ cup shortening or lard
For Double Crust:
2 cups sifted flour
1 tsp. salt
⅔ cup shortening or lard

In a teacup or small bowl, make a paste with ¼ cup of the above flour (⅓ cup if making double crust) and 3 T. water (¼ cup water for double crust). Set in refrigerator. Add salt to the remaining flour and cut shortening into the flour until the size of small peas. Add the water paste to the flour mixture and mix just until dough comes together. Form into a ball and turn out on a floured surface. Roll crust ⅛-inch thick.

Bake pie crust in preheated 425° oven for 12-15 minutes or until golden. (When baking crust empty, put a cup of raw white rice or small white beans into the bottom of the crust, and then bake. The weight from the rice or beans will keep the bottom of the crust from puffing up while baking. You can save the rice or beans to use for future pie crusts by cooling them completely and then storing in an airtight, marked container.)

Notes:

22 Omelet Roll

2 tsp. butter
¼ cup finely diced onion
12 eggs
½ tsp. ground mustard powder
½ tsp. salt
¼ tsp. pepper
½ lb. thinly sliced ham
½ lb. sliced Swiss cheese

Preheat oven to 350°.

Take a large jelly roll pan (at least 10 x 15 inches) and lightly grease bottom and sides. Line the greased pan with parchment or waxed paper; grease the paper.

In a sauté pan, melt butter and add diced onion; cook until onion is limp; set aside.

Combine the eggs, mustard powder, salt, pepper, and onion mixture and whisk well. Pour the mixture into the prepared pan and bake for 10-15 minutes, or until the omelet is set.

Remove omelet from oven and invert onto a piece of aluminum foil; gently peel off parchment paper. Layer the omelet with the ham and Swiss cheese and then roll it up jelly-roll fashion and wrap tightly in aluminum foil.

Place the roll on a cookie sheet and return it to the oven for 10 minutes. When baked, remove the foil, slice the omelet into thick rolls, and serve.

This is a bit fiddly, but the end result is a unique breakfast indulgence.

Notes:

23 Pancakes

1¼ cups flour
1 tsp. sugar
1½ T. baking powder
¾ tsp. salt
⅓ cup butter, melted and cooled slightly
1 cup milk
2 eggs, beaten

Sift together dry ingredients; set aside. In large bowl, mix together in order given the butter, milk, and eggs. Add the sifted dry ingredients and mix just until blended.

Cook pancakes in a lightly oiled frying pan, turning once.

24 Pfannkuchen (Dutch Babies)

½ cup flour
½ tsp. salt
4 eggs
½ cup milk
2-3 T. butter, softened

Preheat oven to 400°.

In a small bowl, stir together the flour and salt.

In a large mixing bowl, beat the eggs thoroughly. Alternately add the flour mixture and milk to the eggs, beating after well each addition— the batter should be smooth.

Spread the softened butter on the bottom and up the sides of a cast iron pot or large ovenproof frying pan. Pour the egg batter into the pot

Notes:

(or frying pan) and set in the oven; bake for 5 minutes and then turn down heat to 350° for another 15-20 minutes or until the pancake is puffed up the sides of the pan and crisp and golden on top.

Serve plain, or with powdered sugar or maple syrup.

Gather the kids around when you take it from the oven because the puffed "baby" is something to behold.

25 Potato Pancakes

3 eggs
6 T. flour
1 tsp. salt
¼ cup milk
5-6 medium-sized potatoes
lard or shortening for frying

In a large bowl, beat the eggs and then add the flour, salt, and milk and whisk to combine.

Peel the raw potatoes and then grate them coarsely. Work quickly so the potatoes don't darken and get starchy. Add the grated potatoes to the egg mixture and stir to mix.

Heat 3-4 tablespoons lard or shortening in a large frying pan and let it melt. Ladle a small amount of the pancake batter (it will be rather runny) into the frying pan and spread each pancake so it's thin. Fry them quickly, turning the pancake over when the first side is crisp and golden. Cook the second side so it's crisp and golden as well.

These pancakes are best eaten as soon as they come out of the pan.

Notes:

26 Pumpkin Pancakes

1 cup flour
⅛ tsp. baking soda
2 T. sugar
¼ tsp. cinnamon
⅛ tsp. ginger
⅛ tsp. nutmeg
1 egg, beaten
1¼ cups milk
2 T. melted shortening, butter, or vegetable oil
½ cup canned pumpkin (can also use cooked, mashed sweet
   potato or Delicata squash)

In a large mixing bowl, mix together the flour, baking soda, sugar, and spices.

In a medium bowl, mix together the egg, milk, melted shortening, and pumpkin. Add to flour mixture and beat well until smooth.

Bake pancakes on a lightly greased griddle or fry pan, turning once. Serve plain, with butter and maple syrup, or with powdered sugar.

Pumpkin pancakes are just the thing on a cold winter morning.

Notes:

27 Sausage, Egg, and Cream of Mushroom Casserole

Start the night before.

2 cups seasoned croutons or cubed dried bread
1 lb. bulk sausage
1 tsp. non-salt seasoning such as Mrs. Dash
4 eggs, beaten
3 cups milk
1 can condensed cream of mushroom soup
1 tsp. ground mustard powder
1 cup cheddar cheese, shredded

Butter a 9 x 13-inch baking dish and spread croutons evenly in the pan.

Brown sausage, drain, and then spread the sausage over the croutons. Sprinkle the non-salt seasoning over that.

Mix together the eggs, milk, soup, and mustard powder and then pour this liquid mixture over the sausage and croutons.

Cover the casserole and refrigerate overnight.

In the morning, let the casserole sit on the counter for 30 minutes while you preheat the oven to 325°. Bake the casserole for 1 hour or until lightly browned. Remove from oven and turn off heat; sprinkle the cheddar cheese over the top and place the casserole back into the oven until cheese has melted.

Let stand for about 5 minutes before serving.

Notes:

28 Sausage and Egg Casserole

Start the night before.

1 lb. bulk pork sausage
6 eggs
1 tsp. dry mustard powder
2 cups milk
1 tsp. salt
6 slices bread, cubed
4 oz. cheddar cheese, cubed or shredded

Brown sausage and drain off grease. Beat the eggs; add mustard, milk, and salt. Mix in the bread cubes, cheese, and sausage. Put in a buttered 9 x 13 or 10 x 15-inch baking dish, cover with plastic wrap, and refrigerate overnight.

In the morning, take the casserole out of the refrigerator and let set on the counter for a half hour while oven is preheating. Bake at 350° for 45-55 minutes or until set. (If you use the smaller baking dish, you'll need to bake it for the longer time.) Remove from the oven and let set for several minutes before cutting.

This dish always gets raves and it's so easy to prepare.

Notes:

29 Scrambled Egg and Ham Bake

Cheese Sauce:
1 T. butter
1½ T. flour
1 cup milk
¼ tsp. salt
pinch of pepper
½-1 cup cheddar cheese, shredded

Filling:
2 T. butter
¾ cup cubed ham
⅛-¼ cup onion, diced (can use green onion if desired)
6 eggs, whisked

Topping:
2-3 T. butter, melted
1 cup soft bread crumbs, heaping

Make cheese sauce: In a medium saucepan, melt butter, blend in flour, and, stirring constantly, slowly pour in milk. Continue stirring until mixture has bubbled and thickened. Add salt, pepper, and cheese and continue stirring until cheese has melted completely. Set aside.

Make filling: In larger frying pan, melt butter. Add ham and onion and sauté until onion is tender. Add whisked eggs and cook, stirring, until eggs are set. Stir in cheese sauce. Set aside.

Make topping: Add bread crumbs to the melted butter and mix well.

Grease a 9 x 9-inch baking dish and spoon egg and cheese mixture evenly in the pan. Sprinkle topping mixture evenly over the top.

Bake at 350° for about 20 minutes or until topping has browned nicely.

Notes:

30 Scrapple

1½ lbs. ground pork or mildly seasoned bulk pork sausage
5 cups water, divided
1 tsp. salt
½ tsp. sage
1 cup cornmeal

Break up ground pork into small pieces in a large saucepan. Add 4 cups of water and stir, separating the pork well. Heat to boiling, reduce to simmer, and cook 30 minutes. Remove meat from stock, reserving 3 cups of the stock. Add the salt and sage to the reserved stock.

Combine the cornmeal with 1 cup cold water (or use half water, half milk, which will make the scrapple brown better when fried). Add this cornmeal/water mixture gradually to the hot stock, stirring while adding; bring to a boil, reduce to simmer, cover, and cook 20 minutes. (If the heat is turned up too high the cornmeal will stick to the bottom of the pot and burn, so be watchful.) Stir in cooked ground pork. Pour into a loaf pan (the kind you would use to bake bread, for instance) and chill well for 24 hours.

Slice ¼ – ½ inch thick. Fry slices in hot oil quickly, turning only once. Make sure there's plenty of room in the pan to turn each slice. Serve plain, with syrup, or with Tomato Gravy (page 37).

I usually use more sage because I love the taste. I use a heavy-bottomed pot for simmering the cornmeal so it doesn't stick as easily. And I use a good amount of oil for frying so the slices get good and crisp. This is the birthday breakfast of choice at our house!

Notes:

31 Tomato Gravy

¼ cup onion, finely diced
2 T. bacon drippings or butter
3 T. flour
1½ cups tomato juice or canned, stewed tomatoes including
    liquid, finely diced
½ cup milk or half and half
2 tsp. brown sugar
salt and pepper to taste

Cook onion in bacon drippings until the onion is golden in color.

Add the flour and stir constantly for 30 seconds. Add the tomato juice or tomatoes and liquid in a steady stream, stirring constantly. Next add the milk or half and half and brown sugar and continue to stir until mixture thickens. Salt and pepper to taste.

Tomato Gravy is tasty served over Scrapple, cornmeal mush, biscuits, or fried eggs and toast.

Notes:

32 Waffles

2 cups sifted flour
2 tsp. baking powder, slightly heaped
2 tsp. sugar
¼ tsp. salt
5 T. butter, melted and then cooled
3 eggs, separated
1½ cups milk

In a medium bowl, beat the egg whites until stiff. Set aside for now. In a large mixing bowl, whisk together the yolks and set aside.

Sift the flour before measuring and then sift together the flour, baking powder, sugar, and salt. (Taking care to sift twice will help ensure your waffles are light and fluffy.)

Alternately add the flour mixture and milk to the egg yolks, mixing well. Add the butter and mix again. Last, fold in the stiffly beaten egg whites.

Cook waffles in a lightly oiled waffle iron.

Notes:

MIDDAY MEALS
AND SNACKS

In times past, the midday meal was called dinner, and rightly so. It was often the large meal of each day, with supper in the evening being comparably light fare—often leftovers. Now, however, most of us are away from home at midday, and we can easily get in the habit of grabbing something and eating on the run.

But that doesn't have to stop you from taking advantage of the hot dishes in this section. If you are home, great. But if you find yourself away from home during the daylight hours, there's no reason why you can't pack your food to go and heat it up when hunger strikes. It may take some advance planning and cooking, but you'll be so glad you made the effort because there's nothing quite as satisfying as a home-cooked meal. And you can save money and eat better into the bargain.

And of course, because this is an Amish cookbook, you'll find more pie recipes throughout the chapter, along with some tasty snacks and quick meal ideas. There's something here for every taste.

Let's dig in!

Dear friend, I pray that you may enjoy
good health and that all may go well with you,
even as your soul is getting along well.

3 JOHN 2

Father, I ask that You would open my heart to the
needs and cares of my loved ones. I'm thankful, Lord,
that one way I can show my love for my family is
through food. Please help me to resist taking shortcuts
where my family's health is concerned. As I cook and
bake, remind me that it's a perfect time to pray for
those I love. The meals I prepare, when drenched in
prayer, can truly be a sacrifice of praise to You. Thank
You that today I will show my love to my family
through the work of my hands. I'm blessed! Amen.

33 Amish Church Spread

½ cup brown sugar
¼ cup water
1 T. butter
2 T. corn syrup
¾ cup peanut butter
½ cup marshmallow cream
½ tsp. vanilla

In a medium saucepan, combine sugar, water, and butter and bring to a boil. Reduce heat to low and then stir in corn syrup; boil for 1 minute more, and then remove from heat. Stir in peanut butter, marshmallow cream, and vanilla and stir with a wooden spoon until well blended. Store in a tightly covered container in the refrigerator until ready to use and then let the spread sit out at room temperature until it's spreadable.

As you can probably imagine, kids love this spread on a piece of toasted or plain bread!

Notes:

34 Apple Crumb Pie

6 apples suitable for pie
1 cup sugar, divided
1 tsp. cinnamon
¾ cup flour
⅓ cup butter
1 unbaked pie shell

Peel and core apples and cut into thin slices. Mix ½ cup sugar with the cinnamon and sprinkle over the apples, gently mixing. Put the apple mixture into the unbaked pie shell.

Using your fingers, blend together the flour, ½ cup sugar, and butter to make coarse crumbs. Sprinkle the crumbs over the apples and bake in a preheated 425° oven for 10 minutes. Reduce the oven to 350° and continue baking for 35 minutes or until pie is done.

This is a tasty variation of the more usual top-crust apple pie. It doesn't take any more time and is a great change of pace.

Notes:

35 Applesauce Loaf Cake

1 cup brown sugar
¼ cup butter
pinch of salt
1 tsp. cinnamon
½ tsp. cloves
pinch of nutmeg
1 cup applesauce
1 tsp. baking soda, dissolved in a small amount of warm water
2 cups flour
1 cup raisins

Frosting:
1 cup powdered sugar
1-2 T. room temperature butter
1 tsp. water

Cream together the sugar, butter, salt, and spices. Add applesauce, dissolved baking soda, and flour; mix well. Add the raisins and mix well again.

Pour batter into a greased loaf pan. Bake at 350° for 45-50 minutes or until done.

Beat together the sugar and butter, adding water if necessary to get desired consistency. Spread on baked and cooled cake.

I usually use fewer raisins, and sometimes I add some chopped nuts.

Notes:

36 Blueberry Custard Pie

1 baked pie shell
1 cup sugar, divided
5 T. cornstarch, divided
⅛ tsp. cinnamon
3 cups blueberries, fresh or frozen
¼ cup orange juice
⅛ tsp. salt
1¼ cups milk
3 eggs, divided

Meringue Topping
3 egg whites (from the divided eggs in pie recipe)
¼ tsp. cream of tartar
6 T. sugar

In a large saucepan, combine ½ cup of the sugar, 3 T. of the cornstarch, and the cinnamon. Stir in blueberries and orange juice. Bring to a boil over medium heat and cook, stirring until thickened (about 2 minutes). Remove from heat and set aside.

In another large saucepan, mix together ½ cup of the sugar, 2 T. of the cornstarch, and salt. Stir in milk until smooth. Cook over medium heat, stirring constantly, until thickened; continue to cook, all the while stirring, for 2 minutes more. Remove from heat, cover, and set aside.

Separate eggs and set whites aside for now. Stir in a small amount of the hot custard mixture into the egg yolks. Stirring constantly, slowly add the egg yolk mixture to the saucepan containing the custard. Bring to a simmer and cook, stirring, for 2 minutes longer. Remove from heat, cover, and set aside.

Notes:

Pour blueberry mixture into the unbaked pie shell. Top with custard mixture.

For the meringue topping: In a large mixing bowl, beat the egg whites and cream of tartar until soft peaks form. Gradually add sugar, 1 tablespoon at a time, beating well after each addition. When done, the meringue will appear glossy and somewhat stiff and peaks will form when beaters are raised. Spread meringue over the custard and pull up into points with a spoon; be careful to bring the meringue to the edges of the crust to seal. Bake at 350° for 12-15 minutes or until meringue is a light golden brown. (Watch carefully because the meringue can quickly go from perfect to dark.)

Serve at room temperature. Meringue doesn't take well to refrigeration, so plan to eat it the same day.

Notes:

37 Cabbage Chowder

3 cups water, more or less
4 cups cabbage, coarsely shredded
2 cups carrots, peeled and sliced
3 cups potatoes, peeled and diced
1 T. salt
½ tsp. sugar
¼ tsp. pepper
¼ tsp. caraway seeds
4 cups scalded milk
2 T. butter

Cook the vegetables and seasonings in just enough water to cover; add a bit more water if necessary while cooking to keep them covered. When the vegetables are cooked tender, add the scalded milk and butter and heat thoroughly, but don't boil.

When serving, you can also sprinkle a bit of shredded cheddar or Monterey jack cheese on top.

Notes:

38 Caramel Corn

6 quarts popped corn (about ¾ cup unpopped corn)
1 cup peanuts (or other nuts), optional
1 cup butter
2 cups firmly packed brown sugar
½ cup corn syrup
1 tsp. salt
½ tsp. baking soda

Preheat oven to 250°.

Butter or spray with oil a very large mixing bowl and two rimmed large jelly-roll pans. Place the popped corn and peanuts into the greased mixing bowl and set aside for now.

In a medium saucepan combine the butter, brown sugar, corn syrup, and salt. Bring to a boil over medium heat, stirring constantly. Lower heat and let the mixture boil for 5 minutes without stirring.

Remove saucepan from heat and stir in the baking soda. (When you add the baking soda, the syrup will froth and grow for a few moments so don't be concerned when your syrup temporarily acts like a mini volcano.) Gradually pour the syrup over the popped corn, mixing well to coat all the kernels. (I use a very large wooden spoon and it seems to work well.) Spread the caramel corn evenly into the two prepared jelly-roll pans. Bake the caramel corn for up to an hour, stirring every 15 minutes. Or don't bake at all and dig right in!

Notes:

39 Chewy Oatmeal Cookies

1 cup butter, room temperature
1 cup granulated sugar, plus a bit more for rolling
1 cup brown sugar
2 eggs
1 tsp. vanilla
2 cups flour
1 tsp. baking soda
1 scant tsp. salt
1½ tsp. ground cinnamon
¼ tsp. ground cardamom seed
¼ tsp. ground nutmeg
3 cups rolled oats

In a large mixing bowl, beat together the butter and sugars. Add eggs one at a time, beating well after each addition. Stir in vanilla.

In another, smaller bowl, combine flour, baking soda, salt, and spices. Add to the creamed mixture and stir well. Add oats and mix well again. Cover bowl and chill for at least an hour.

Roll dough into balls and roll the balls in granulated sugar. Place dough balls 2 inches apart on greased cookie sheet. Flatten slightly. (Instead of rolling the dough balls in sugar, you can place them on the greased cookie sheet and then dip a fork into the sugar and flatten cookies slightly, running the fork across the tops to release the sugar.)

Bake at 375° for 8-10 minutes.

Notes:

40 Chocolate Sauce

1½ cups water
3 cups sugar
1½ cups cocoa powder
¼ tsp. salt
1 tsp. vanilla
2 T. corn syrup

In a small bowl, mix together the cocoa powder and salt; set aside.

In a 3- or 4-quart pot, mix together the water and sugar. Turn heat to medium and heat to boiling, whisking constantly. Once the sugar water is boiling, add the remainder of the ingredients, whisking constantly. (Note that when the cocoa powder is added, the mixture will bubble up in the pot.)

Lower the heat and continue to whisk and cook the sauce for about 15 minutes; the liquid will be reduced and the sauce will thicken slightly.

Cool and use it over ice cream, fruit, cake, or mixed with milk for chocolate milk or hot chocolate.

You can also water-bath can the chocolate sauce. Use half-pint or 4-ounce canning jars and process for 15 minutes. (My book *The Amish Canning Cookbook* has up-to-date guidelines for safe processing.)

Part of what I love about this recipe is that all the ingredients can usually be found on my pantry shelves. Love that!

Notes:

41 Coffee Cake

Coffee Cake:
1¼ cups flour
½ cup sugar
2 tsp. baking powder
½ tsp. salt
½ cup milk
1 egg
3 T. butter, melted and cooled

Cinnamon Nut Topping:
¼ cup brown sugar
¼ cup chopped nuts
1 T. flour
2 tsp. ground cinnamon
1 T. butter, room temperature

Prepare Cinnamon Nut Topping: In a small mixing bowl, mix together the brown sugar, chopped nuts, flour, and cinnamon; add butter and mix together until mixture resembles coarse crumbs; set aside for now.

Prepare Coffee Cake: In a large mixing bowl, stir together flour, sugar, baking powder, and salt. Pour milk into another bowl; stir in egg and melted butter. Pour all at once into the flour mixture and stir just until mixed. Pour batter into a greased 8 x 8-inch baking dish. Sprinkle the Cinnamon Nut Topping over the top of the batter and bake at 375° for 20-25 minutes or until baked through.

This is a rather plain Jane coffee cake, but it's so good that you'll turn to this recipe again and again. It's also excellent without nuts.

Notes:

42 Corn Bread

1 cup flour
¼ cup sugar
1 T. baking powder
¾ tsp. salt
1 cup cornmeal
1 egg, well beaten
1 cup milk
5 T. shortening, melted and cooled

Sift together the flour, sugar, baking powder, and salt. Mix in cornmeal.

Blend together the egg, milk, and melted shortening; add to dry ingredients and beat until smooth.

Grease the bottom only of an 8 x 8-inch baking dish and pour in batter. Bake at 400° for 20 minutes or until bread is done and begins to pull away from the sides of the pan.

Notes:

43 Cornflake Baked Chicken

⅓ cup mayonnaise
½ tsp. salt
½ tsp. garlic salt
½ tsp. rosemary
1 frying chicken, 3-3½ lbs., cut into pieces
1½ cups crushed cornflakes

In a bowl, mix together the mayonnaise, salt, garlic salt, and rosemary. Brush pieces of chicken with the mayonnaise mixture and then roll them in the crushed cornflakes.

Place the chicken, skin side up, in a lightly greased baking pan; don't crowd the pieces. Bake uncovered in a 350° oven for 1 hour or until all chicken pieces are thoroughly cooked.

I've used this recipe with boneless, skinless chicken breasts with great success, although I reduce the bake time by about 20 minutes. How long you bake the chicken is contingent upon the size of the individual pieces.

Notes:

44 Cottage Cheese

1 gallon milk
⅓ cup white vinegar
salt to taste
cream or half and half to taste

Pour the milk into a large, nonreactive pot (such as stainless steel) and slowly heat the milk to 180-190° F. (No need to stir.) When the milk has reached the proper temperature, remove from the heat and add the vinegar. Stir to mix and then let the mixture set for about 30 minutes or until the curds and whey completely separate.

Pour the curds and whey into a colander that has been lined with a double thickness of cheesecloth. Allow the whey to drain completely, about 15 minutes. Wrap the cheesecloth around the curds and rinse with cool tap water for several minutes, gently kneading the curds as you rinse. Drain again and then place the curds in a bowl. Add some cream or half and half and salt to taste.

Note: You can use the whey to replace milk or water (there will be a lot!) in many recipes, such as biscuits, bread, cornbread, cooked oatmeal, and even smoothies. But remember that the whey from this recipe is acidic from use of the vinegar, so it will add a tangy taste to your food.

Note: In this recipe, low-fat or nonfat milk works well. I think it makes the curds "curdier."

Making cottage cheese is quick and easy!

Notes:

45 Cottage Cheese Pancakes

1 cup cottage cheese
4 eggs
½ cup flour
¼ tsp. salt
¼ cup oil
½ cup milk
½ tsp. vanilla, optional

Mix together all ingredients until well blended and batter is smooth, although there will still be small lumps of cottage cheese. Fry on lightly greased griddle or frying pan; leave plenty of room between pancakes for turning…and turn quick because the batter is thin, but you'll soon get the hang of it.

If you've ever eaten cheese blintzes or crepes, these pancakes will prove reminiscent. Not really a pancake, per se, these delicate pancakes make for an excellent light brunch or lunch when paired with a tossed green salad or fruit. Or try them rolled around a bit of blackberry jam and then sprinkled with powdered sugar. I make these for breakfast, lunch, and sometimes even dinner because they're just that good!

Notes:

46 Dutch Meat Loaf

2½ lb. ground beef
2½ cups bread crumbs
1 cup cheese, coarse shred or finely cubed
¼ cup green pepper, diced
¼ cup onion, diced
2 eggs
1 cup catsup
salt and pepper to taste

In a large bowl and using your fingers, mix together all ingredients, reserving ½ cup catsup for the top. Form meat into two loaves and put them in loaf pans. Spread the remaining catsup over the tops and bake at 350° for 1 hour and 15 minutes or until done.

47 Dutch Slaw

1 head cabbage
½ cup cream
1 tsp. salt
½ cup sugar
½ cup vinegar

Discard outer leaves of cabbage. Wash the remainder of the cabbage, drain well, and then shred leaves.

Mix together the cream, salt, sugar, and vinegar and beat very well.

Just before serving, combine the cabbage and dressing and mix well.

This is classic coleslaw to my way of thinking. If desired, you can add a bit of diced onion, carrot, or bell pepper. For a change of pace, I sometimes add a can of drained mandarin oranges. Delicious!

Notes:

48 Five-Hour Beef Stew

2 lb. beef stew meat, cubed
3 onions, chopped
6 carrots, chopped
1 cup celery, chopped
2 cups peas, fresh or frozen
1 28-ounce can tomatoes, including liquid
2 T. tapioca
½ T. sugar
1 T. salt
1 slice stale bread, torn into small pieces
4 potatoes, peeled and cubed

Mix together all ingredients. Place in a large covered casserole dish (about 3-quart size). Bake at 250° for 5 hours.

This stew is perfect for those days when you're busy and don't want to fuss in the kitchen.

Notes:

49 Fruit Cream Pie

You can use almost any fruit for this pie. My favorites are blackberry, blueberry, cherry, currant, raspberry, and strawberry.

1 unbaked pie shell
½ cup sugar
1 tsp. flour
½ tsp. salt
3 eggs, beaten
2½ cups milk
½-¾ cup fruit

In a large heatproof mixing bowl stir together the sugar, flour, and salt. Add the beaten eggs and stir again.

Bring the milk to almost boiling and then slowly add it to the egg mixture, stirring constantly. Pour it into the unbaked pie shell and sprinkle the fruit over the top. Bake at 350° for about 45 minutes or until the custard is set. Cool.

You can serve this plain, or top with meringue or sweetened whipped cream.

Notes:

50 German Potato Salad

8 potatoes, peeled, cubed, and boiled
1 stalk celery, chopped
2 hard-boiled eggs
1 onion, chopped
1 T. fresh parsley, minced

Dressing
4 slices bacon, diced
2 eggs, well beaten
1 cup sugar
½ cup vinegar
½ cup cold water
¼ tsp. dry mustard
½ tsp. salt
¼ tsp. pepper

Combine all salad ingredients in large bowl and then prepare dressing.

Fry bacon in a skillet until crisp. Remove the bacon bits and add to salad. Beat together eggs, sugar, vinegar, water, and spices. Pour mixture into the hot bacon grease and cook, stirring, until mixture thickens, about 10 minutes. Pour over the potato mixture and mix gently. Refrigerate for several hours before serving, or eat when it's cooled down to room temperature.

Notes:

51 Ham and Noodle Bake

2 cups uncooked egg noodles
1½ cups cooked ham, diced
3 eggs, beaten
1½ cups milk
salt and pepper to taste

Cook the noodles in plenty of boiling salted water until done; drain them in a colander.

In a heavily greased 9 x 13-inch baking dish, layer the noodles and ham.

Beat together the eggs, milk, salt, and pepper; pour over the noodles and ham.

Bake at 350° for 30 minutes.

MIDDAY MEALS AND SNACKS

Notes:

52 Hog Maw (Stuffed Pig's Stomach)

1 pig's stomach
2 lbs. fresh bulk sausage, smoked if you can get it
4 cups potatoes, peeled and diced
1 cup apples, pared, cored, and chopped
2½ cups bread cubes
1 medium onion, chopped
1 cup celery, diced
1 cup carrots, peeled and sliced
¼ cup fresh parsley, chopped
salt and pepper to taste

If you butcher your own hogs, you're in luck—but most of us will need to locate a pig stomach, and it's not likely the local grocery store carries them. Ask a local butcher or local hog farmer.

Soak the pig stomach in lightly salted water; rinse and remove as much fat as possible while cleaning; pat dry.

Combine the remaining ingredients, breaking up the sausage meat as you work, and mix well. Stuff the stomach with as much of the mixture as you can, pressing well after each addition (the pig stomach will stretch). Sew up opening with baker's twine or heavy-duty sewing thread.

Place the stuffed stomach in a heavy ovenproof pot, add ½ cup water or broth, cover tightly, and bake at 350° for 2 hours. Baste with the pan juices occasionally, and add another ½ cup water or broth about halfway through baking if it looks too dry. Remove cover and bake another 15 minutes or so.

If the thought of eating stuffed pig's stomach is disagreeable, remember that in some circles, this is quite a delicacy, and people have been eating hog maw for a very long time. But if you're still squeamish, you can always scoop the dressing away from the lining and eat it sans maw.

Notes:

53 Homemade Egg Noodles

1 cup flour
½ tsp. salt
2 eggs, beaten

In a mixing bowl, stir together the flour and salt. Make a well in the middle and add the eggs. Start mixing the flour into the eggs (use a fork for this) and keep incorporating more of the flour into the dough until it forms a ball; it will be sticky but should stick together.

Turn out dough ball onto a floured surface and keep adding in more of the flour, kneading as you go. You want the dough to be smooth and no longer sticky, but not too dry. Wrap the dough in plastic wrap and chill in the refrigerator for 30 minutes. (Many times I've been in a hurry and don't chill my dough and I don't seem to have problems. If you're going to stint due to time constraints, better to stint here than forgo the drying time after the noodles are cut.)

Remove the chilled dough, place it back on the floured work surface, and cut into two pieces. Working with one half at a time and keeping the other half wrapped, roll out the dough as thin as you desire, and then cut the dough into noodles. Let the noodles sit on a drying rack for about 30 minutes or so until ready to cook.

To cook the noodles, bring a large pot of salted water to a good boil. Drop in the noodles and cook until done, stirring occasionally. The boiling time will vary, but you can figure somewhere between 5 and 10 minutes, depending on how thick the noodles are.

Notes:

54 Homemade Pasta Noodles (No Eggs)

2 cups semolina flour*
½ tsp. salt
½ cup warm water

In a mixing bowl, stir together the flour and salt. Make a well in the center and pour the warm water into the well. Using a fork, incorporate the flour into the water. Keep mixing until a ball forms. Turn out the ball of dough (it will be sticky) onto a floured surface and knead gently for 10 minutes. Use more flour to keep the dough from sticking, but try to use as little as possible. If the dough becomes too dry, sprinkle on a few drops of warm water and keep kneading. Wrap the dough in plastic wrap and let it rest for 20 minutes; then set the ball of dough, still tightly wrapped, into the refrigerator for 30 minutes.

Tear or cut the dough into 4 equal pieces and work with one piece at a time, keeping the others wrapped and in the refrigerator so they don't dry out. On a lightly floured surface, roll the dough out and cut into noodles.

To cook the pasta, drop noodles into boiling, salted water and cook for about 3-5 minutes or until done.

---

* Semolina flour is made from coarse grinding Durham wheat berries. You can use other kinds of flour, including all-purpose and whole wheat, but Semolina/Durham flour makes the very best pasta noodles. When we were kids growing up, Mama would sometimes use Cream of Wheat cereal straight from the box in lieu of the more expensive Semolina to make our noodles. It works very well!

Notes:

55 Huntington Casserole

4 T. butter
4 T. flour
1 cup milk
2 cups chicken broth
2 cups cooked, diced chicken
2 cups uncooked egg noodles
1 cup cheddar cheese, shredded
Cracker crumbs, bread crumbs, or crushed potato chips

Butter or grease a 9 x 9-inch casserole.

In a medium saucepan, melt butter; add the flour and whisk until blended. Add the milk and then the broth in a stream, whisking constantly. Keep whisking and cooking until the white sauce thickens; remove from heat.

In a large bowl (or the saucepan if it's large enough), gently mix together all ingredients except cracker crumbs. Mix as little as possible so that the chicken doesn't shred. (Overmixing will do that.) Spoon mixture into prepared dish, top with the cracker crumbs, and bake in a preheated 350° oven for 35-45 minutes, or until casserole is bubbly and cooked through.

Notes:

56 Old-Fashioned Beef Pot Pie

2 lbs. stewing beef, cubed
6 potatoes, chopped or thinly sliced
2 onions, chopped or thinly sliced
¼ cup fresh parsley, chopped fine (or use ⅛ cup dried)
pot pie dough squares (see below)
salt and pepper to taste

In a large pot, add beef cubes and enough water to cover. Season with a bit of salt and pepper and boil beef until tender; add more water if necessary—don't boil dry. When meat is tender, remove from broth and set aside for now.

Peel and cut potatoes and onions; set aside for now.

For the pot pie dough: Add a pinch of salt to 2 cups flour. Add 1 beaten egg and enough flour to make a stiff dough. Roll out dough as thin as possible on a floured surface and then cut into 2-inch squares.

Now assemble the pot pie: Into the hot broth, make layers of potatoes, onions, parsley and pot pie squares. Repeat layers, ending with pot pie squares on top.

Cover the pot and simmer for 20 minutes; don't lift cover! After the pot-pie is cooked, return the meat to the pot and cook on low just until the meat is heated through.

Many of us think *meat pie* when we hear the words "pot pie." This version of pot pie doesn't use a crust and is more like a meat and noodle squares dish. It is—to my way of thinking, at least—more traditional.

Notes:

57 Orange Cream Jell-O

2½ cups water
1 box orange Jell-O
2 boxes vanilla instant pudding
1 can mandarin oranges, drained
2 cups lightly sweetened whipped cream

Bring water to a boil; remove from heat. Add the Jell-O and stir until dissolved. Add the pudding and stir thoroughly. Cool until thickened slightly; add the mandarin oranges and whipped cream and stir to mix well. Refrigerate until fully set.

Notes:

58 Potato Stuffing

6 cups mashed potatoes, room temperature
3 eggs, beaten
1 quart bread cubes
1 stick (½ cup) butter
½ cup onion, minced
1 cup celery, diced
½ cup fresh parsley, minced
salt and pepper to taste

In a large mixing bowl stir together the mashed potatoes and beaten eggs.

In a large saucepan, melt the butter; sauté the onion and celery. Add the bread cubes and toast for several minutes, carefully and constantly stirring. Remove from the heat, and add the parsley and salt and pepper.

Combine the bread mixture with the mashed potato mixture and mix thoroughly. Spread in a large, greased roasting pan; sprinkle with paprika and pats of butter if desired. Bake at 350° for 1 hour, or until the stuffing is baked through and the top is golden.

Notes:

59 Pumpkin Bread

3 cups sugar
1 cup oil
4 eggs, beaten
2 cups canned pumpkin (or 1 can if using store-bought canned
    pumpkin)
3½ cups flour
⅔ cup water
1½ tsp. salt
½ tsp. cloves
1 tsp. each cinnamon, allspice, nutmeg

Mix together the sugar, oil, and eggs. Add pumpkin and stir to mix.
Add the dry ingredients and the water and stir just until mixed.

Pour batter into two greased and floured loaf pans and bake at 350°
for 1 hour.

This bread is good plain, toasted with butter, or spread with cream
cheese.

MIDDAY MEALS AND SNACKS

Notes:

60 Quick German Sweet Rolls

4½ cups flour, divided
1 tsp. salt
1 cup granulated sugar
1 tsp. baking soda
2 tsp. cream of tartar
½ cup lard or shortening
½ cup butter
2 eggs
¼ cup milk
¼ cup water
1 cup brown sugar

In a large mixing bowl, sift together 4 cups of the flour, salt, granulated sugar, baking soda, and cream of tartar. Cut in lard and butter until mixture resembles coarse crumbs. Add 1 well-beaten egg, milk, and water and mix to form a soft dough.

In another bowl, mix together 1 beaten egg, brown sugar, and ½ cup flour.

Roll dough to ½-inch thickness and spread with the brown sugar mixture. Roll up jelly-roll style and cut into inch-thick slices. Place slices 2 inches apart on greased baking sheets.

Bake at 375° for 8 to 10 minutes.

Notes:

61 Sand Tarts

1 cup butter
¾ cup powdered sugar, more or less
1 tsp. vanilla
2 cups flour
1 cup chopped walnuts

In a large mixing bowl, beat the butter until light and smooth. Add ½ cup powdered sugar and vanilla and beat well again. Add flour and mix until blended; stir in nuts.

Shape the dough into a flattened ball. Wrap tightly in plastic wrap and refrigerate until cold.

Line cookie sheets with parchment paper. Shape dough into 1-inch balls and place on the prepared cookie sheets. Bake at 325° for 20 minutes, or until golden brown and baked through.

While the first batch of cookies is baking, sift ¼ cup powdered sugar into a bowl. When the cookies are removed from the oven and while still warm, roll them in the powdered sugar and cool on wire rack.

Notes:

62 Schmeirkase

Schmeirkase is a spreadable cheese similar to cream cheese, sometimes called "spread cheese" or "spoon cheese."

1 quart milk (raw if you can get it)
1 quart boiling water
2 T. milk, or to taste
2 T. cream, or to taste
½ tsp. salt

Pour milk into an earthenware bowl or other nonreactive container; let stand in a warm place until thick and sour. (I put it in my oven with the oven light on.)

When the milk has soured and is quite thick, pour boiling water over it. Let the mixture stand for several minutes and then pour into a large cheesecloth bag (use double layers); drain overnight or for about 12 hours.

Beat well, adding milk, cream, and salt. The cheese should end up the consistency of thick apple butter.

Spread schmeirkase on toasted bagels or bread. You can also add spices such as caraway seeds, garlic, parsley, or chives and serve it with crackers or raw vegetables.

Notes:

63 Shoofly Pie

1 unbaked pie crust

Crumbs
½ cup butter or shortening
1½ cups flour
1 cup brown sugar
½ tsp. cinnamon

Syrup
½ cup molasses
1 tsp. baking soda
1 cup boiling water
⅛ tsp. salt
pinch of nutmeg, ginger, cinnamon, and cloves

Preheat oven to 450°. With your fingers or a fork, mix together all of the crumb ingredients until coarse crumbs form; set aside.

Make the syrup: In a heatproof saucepan or mixing bowl, stir to dissolve the baking soda in the molasses; add the boiling water, salt, and spices and stir well.

Pour one-third of the syrup into the bottom of the pie shell; add a third of the crumbs; repeat these layers twice more, ending with the crumbs.

Place the pie into the oven and immediately turn down heat to 350°. Bake for 30-35 minutes or until the crumbs and crust are golden.

Notes:

64 Soft Molasses Cookies

1 cup butter, room temperature
1½ cups sugar
½ cup molasses
2 eggs
4 cups flour
½ tsp. salt
2¼ tsp. baking soda
2 tsp. ginger
1 tsp. cloves
1½ tsp. cinnamon
extra sugar, for rolling

Cream together the butter and sugar. Add molasses and eggs and beat well. Add flour, salt, baking soda, and spices; beat again. Chill at least 30 minutes. Roll dough into balls and then roll balls in sugar and place on ungreased cookie sheet.

Bake at 350° for 10-11 minutes. Do not overbake.

Notes:

65 Tomato Soup

This soup recipe is so easy and quick. You start with a can of tomato paste and you end up 20 minutes later with a delicious soup for just pennies a serving. Serve it with crackers or grilled cheese sandwiches and enjoy homemade comfort food!

1 6-oz. can tomato paste
1 quart water
1 stalk celery, chunked into thirds
½ tsp. salt, or to taste
¼ tsp. onion powder
⅛ tsp. each garlic powder, oregano, basil, thyme, rosemary, and
    celery seed
1 bay leaf
1 T. butter
1 T. flour
¼-½ cup milk

In a pot, mix together all ingredients except for the butter, flour, and milk. Simmer for 20 minutes. Remove celery pieces and bay leaf and turn down heat to low.

In a small saucepan, melt the butter and then whisk in the flour. Slowly add ½ cup of the soup, whisking constantly while adding. When the roux is smooth, add about another ½ cup of soup, continuing to whisk. Now slowly pour roux into the soup, whisking all the while. The soup will thicken slightly after a minute or so. Just before ready to serve, add the milk and stir.

This soup is excellent plain, but it's also tasty with a dollop of sour cream on top.

Notes:

66 Whole Wheat Bread

This recipe makes one loaf.

1 cup warm water
½ tsp. sugar
3 tsp. yeast
¼ cup milk
2 T. shortening or butter
2 T. honey
½ tsp. salt
3 tsp. vital wheat gluten
3½ cups whole wheat flour, divided

Place warm water in a large mixing bowl. Add sugar and yeast; mix so yeast gets wet and then let it sit for about 10 minutes or until the mixture is bubbly.

In the meantime, put milk and shortening or butter in a small saucepan and gently heat it until warm; the shortening or butter may not be entirely melted. (You can also place the milk and shortening into a microwavable container and microwave it for about 30 seconds.) Let the mixture cool a tad while you're waiting for the yeast mixture to bubble.

Now, pour the milk/shortening mixture into the large mixing bowl that contains the yeast mixture. Add honey, salt, vital wheat gluten, and about 1 cup whole wheat flour. Mix together; keep adding flour and mixing (you'll use somewhere around 3½ cups flour total, including what you use while kneading to keep things from sticking) until the dough tends to stay in a ball and leave the sides of the bowl. Then turn the dough ball out onto a floured surface and knead for 8-10 minutes; keep adding flour to your work surface so the dough doesn't stick while you work it.

Notes:

Grease another large clean bowl and plop your kneaded ball of dough into it, turning the dough so all surfaces are greased. Cover with a clean towel and let it rise until doubled. Punch down the dough, form it into a ball again, and put it back in the bowl to rise a second time (make sure the surface of the dough is greased again). After the dough has doubled a second time, punch it down and form it into a loaf. Place it into a greased loaf pan and let rise again. This time, let the dough rise until it's about an inch above the top of the loaf pan at its tallest point.

Bake in a preheated 375° oven for about 35 minutes. When it's done, take it out of the loaf pan and let the bread cool on a rack.

Notes:

QUICK AND EASY DINNERS

Dinnertime. It's a chance for families to sit down together and talk about their day while sharing a home-cooked meal. If you are a family with older children, it might seem almost impossible to gather everyone around the table, but don't give up! Establish a pattern of family dinners early on, and then work hard to maintain the habit as the years go by. Even if your teens don't seem overjoyed to be at the table night after night, in a few years those memories are likely to become fond ones.

It's also true that our days often start early and we go full-speed through them. So by the time we need to prepare the evening meal, we're tired. The recipes in this section are quick and easy, and many of them can be prepared ahead of time, refrigerated, and then baked later. Just make sure you add a few minutes onto the cook time if needed to compensate for the cold start.

You'll find several more pie recipes tucked into these pages—the Apple Pie with Buttered Walnut Topping is a particularly good twist on an American classic. And then there's always Potato Rivvel Soup—a hearty, kid-friendly, and budget-friendly meal sure to warm you and your loved ones on cold winter evenings.

So pull up a chair and dig in!

*A person can do nothing better than to eat and
drink and find satisfaction in their own toil.
This too, I see, is from the hand of God.*

ECCLESIASTES 2:24

*Dearest Father, thank You for today. As evening approaches,
keep me cheerfully focused on my loved ones. Our
days can sometimes be long and tiring, but when we
remember to include You in our activities and prayers,
You lovingly shoulder our cares. How wonderful is that!
Help me remember that the bonds of family are sacred
to You, Lord, and should not be broken, even as we live
in this broken world. Remind me daily of my many
blessings so I can be a blessing to those I love. Amen.*

67 Apple Crisp

1 cup brown sugar, packed
1 cup flour
2 tsp. cinnamon, divided
½ cup cold butter
2½ lbs. apples (about 7 or 8)
2 tsp. lemon juice

Lightly grease or butter a 9-inch square baking dish; set aside.

In a small mixing bowl, stir together sugar, flour, and 1 tsp. cinnamon. With a pastry blender or your fingers, cut in butter until mixture is crumbly; set aside.

In another mixing bowl, peel, core, and thinly slice the apples. Add the remaining 1 tsp. cinnamon and lemon juice; gently mix. Spread the apples in the prepared baking dish and sprinkle crumb mixture evenly over the top.

Bake uncovered in a preheated 350° oven for 50-60 minutes or until apples are tender and the crumb topping is golden and crisp. Let cool for about 30 minutes and then serve.

During apple season, this is an easy go-to recipe when you want a quick and satisfying dessert. Get a head start by mixing up several batches of the crumb topping ahead of time, put them in tightly covered canning jars or plastic bags, and refrigerate them until needed. They'll keep just fine for a week or so.

QUICK AND EASY DINNERS

Notes:

68 Apple Pie with Buttered Walnut Toffee Topping

Pie
Pastry for a 2-crust pie
⅓ cup light corn syrup
3 T. sugar
1 T. butter, melted
1 T. quick-cooking tapioca
1 tsp. cinnamon
½ tsp. nutmeg
¼ tsp. salt
4-6 apples, peeled, cored, and thinly sliced (I used Granny Smiths, but any good pie apple will work)

Buttered Walnut Toffee Topping
½ cup brown sugar, slightly heaping
¼ cup chopped walnuts or pecans
3 T. light corn syrup
3 T. butter, melted
1 tsp. vanilla
2 T. flour
¼ tsp. cinnamon

Roll out half of the dough and line a large pie plate. (Use at least a 9.5-inch size or you'll have boil-over issues. I personally use a large, extra deep pie plate and don't have boil-overs.) Set aside for now.

Preheat oven to 425°.

In a large mixing bowl, combine the corn syrup, sugar, melted butter, tapioca, cinnamon, nutmeg, and salt; mix and let set for 10 minutes. Add the sliced apples and mix to coat. Place filling in pie shell. Roll out

Notes:

the top crust and place on top of the apple mixture. Crimp the edges, making sure that there is a ridge all around the edge of the crust. This will be very helpful when you add the toffee topping later on. Make some slashes in the top crust to help steam vent.

Bake at 425° for 10 minutes and then reduce the heat to 350° and bake for another 30 minutes.

While pie is baking make the buttered walnut toffee topping as follows:

Mix together all of the topping ingredients. Remove the pie from the oven after the above baking time is complete and pour topping over the top crust. (You'll find that the topping doesn't "pour" too well, but just do your best to cover the whole area.) Immediately return the pie into the oven, still set at 350°, and bake for 5 more minutes. If you are worried about the pie boiling over, try placing a large cookie sheet underneath to catch drips.

Remove pie from the oven and place on a rack to cool. It needs to cool until almost room temperature before you slice into it so the butter toffee coating has a chance to harden.

This recipe gives a whole new meaning to apple pie. It's delectable. Try topping the pie with pecans instead of walnuts for a tasty variation.

Notes:

69 Baked Beans

2 cups dried navy (small white) beans
½ lb. bacon, diced
½ cup catsup
1 medium onion, chopped
1½ T. salt
1 cup brown sugar
½ cup granulated sugar
1 pint tomato juice

Place beans in a large stockpot and add enough water to cover. Boil for 5 minutes, cover the pot, and let sit for 1 hour. Drain the beans and cover them again with fresh water. Place them back on the stove and simmer until they are cooked, about 2 hours, adding boiling water as needed to keep them covered. When the beans are tender, drain most of the water off and then add the remainder of the ingredients; stir to mix thoroughly.

Spread mixture in a large bean pot or ovenproof casserole and bake at 350°, uncovered, for about 2 hours, adding a bit of boiling water if needed so they don't dry out and scorch on the bottom.

Baked beans are...well...*baked.* But I confess that we sometimes eat this without baking because we like our beans runny. So suit yourself: bake them for the allotted time, bake them for half the time, or don't bake them at all. They'll be good no matter what you decide.

Notes:

70 Beef and Biscuit Casserole

Buttermilk Biscuits, unbaked (see recipe on page 17)
1½ lbs. hamburger
½ cup onion, chopped
4 oz. cream cheese
¼ cup milk
1 can cream of mushroom soup
1 tsp. salt
½ cup catsup

Brown the hamburger and onions; drain. Mix meat mixture with
the cream cheese, milk, cream of mushroom soup, salt, and catsup.
Spread into a lightly buttered baking dish and bake at 375° for 15
minutes. Place the unbaked biscuits on top, leaving room between
them to rise while baking. Return to the oven and bake for about 20
minutes or until the biscuits are done and golden on top. Times will
vary depending on size of biscuits.

Notes:

71 Butterscotch Pie with Meringue Topping

¼ cup butter
1 cup firmly packed brown sugar
¼ cup flour
2 cups milk, divided
3 egg yolks (reserve the egg whites for the meringue topping)
½ tsp. vanilla
pinch of salt
1 pie shell, baked and cooled

Meringue Topping
3 egg whites
½ tsp. vanilla
¼ tsp. cream of tartar
6 T. sugar

In a medium saucepan over medium-low heat, stir the brown sugar and butter until butter melts and sugar dissolves. Continue stirring and cook mixture for 2 minutes longer; remove from heat.

In a small bowl, beat egg yolks well; set aside for now.

In a large mixing bowl, combine the flour and 1 cup of the milk, mixing until smooth. Add the egg yolks and salt and mix well again. Add the remaining milk and thoroughly blend.

Return the sugar and butter mixture to the stove and cook on medium-low heat, slowly adding the flour mixture and stirring constantly the entire time. Continue to stir constantly until the mixture is thickened—don't rush this step and keep the heat low. Remove from heat and add the vanilla. Continue to stir the caramel syrup while it cools to barely warm and then pour into the prepared pie shell.

QUICK AND EASY DINNERS

Notes:

Top pie with meringue (see instructions below), being careful to seal the edges. Take the back of a spoon and lift up peaks or make swirls across the top. Bake in a preheated 350° oven for 12-15 minutes or until meringue is golden. Allow pie to cool before serving.

Prepare the meringue topping: In a medium mixing bowl beat the egg whites together with the vanilla and cream of tartar until soft peaks form. Gradually add the sugar, beating hard until stiff and glossy peaks form and all the sugar is dissolved. Top pie with meringue as directed above.

Notes:

72 Cabbage Patch Stew

1 lb. hamburger
1 cup onions, chopped
2 carrots, peeled and sliced
2 ribs celery, sliced
1½ cups coarsely chopped cabbage
2 cans diced or stewed tomatoes, undrained
1 can pinto or kidney beans, rinsed and drained
1 cup water or beef broth, plus more as needed
1 tsp. salt
¼ tsp. pepper
1-2 tsp. chili powder

In a large pot, brown the hamburger; drain off fat. Add the rest of the ingredients, cover, and simmer for about 45 minutes or until vegetables are cooked through and tender. Add more broth or water as needed so the stew doesn't dry out.

Serve in bowls topped with shredded cheddar cheese and sour cream if desired.

Variation: Prepare a batch of biscuit dough (see page 17 for a great biscuit recipe or use your own); making sure there is plenty of broth in the stew, pour the stew into a large baking dish. Top the stew with the cutout biscuits and bake at 375° for about 20-25 minutes or until biscuits are done and golden on top.

Notes:

73 Candied Apples

10-15 apples, depending on size (tart, firm-fleshed apples work best)
Popsicle or craft sticks
2 cups sugar
1 cup corn syrup
1½ cups water
8 drops red food coloring

Wash apples and dry completely. Remove stems and insert one stick into each apple at the stem end.

Lightly grease a cookie sheet and set aside for now. Alternatively, you can use a silicon baking sheet, but there's no need to prepare the surface.

In a medium saucepan (it can't be too small because the liquid will bubble up when boiling), on medium-high heat, mix together the sugar, corn syrup, and water. Stir until sugar is dissolved and then let the mixture come to a boil without stirring until heat reaches 300-310°. Remove from heat and stir in food coloring.

Working with one apple at a time and holding it carefully by the stick handle so you don't get burned, dip and swirl the apple into the candy syrup mixture to evenly coat. Place apples on the greased cookie sheet or on the silicon baking sheeting and allow to rest until candy shell has hardened.

Notes:

74 Chicken un Kraut

1 roasting chicken, 3-4 lbs. (you can use a young duck if you
    prefer)
1 onion, quartered
2 quarts sauerkraut
1 cup water
2 T. sugar

Preheat oven to 450°.

Place chicken in a roasting pan; sprinkle with salt and pepper. Stuff
the cavity with the onion. Add the sauerkraut and water around
the chicken. Sprinkle sugar over the sauerkraut; cover and place the
chicken in the oven, reducing the heat to 375°. Bake until chicken
is cooked through and tender and juices run clear, about 1½ hours.

75 Chocolate Oatmeal Revel Bars

Dough
1 cup butter
2 cups brown sugar
2 eggs
½ tsp. salt
1 tsp. baking soda
3 cups rolled oats
2½ cups flour

Notes:

Filling
2 cups chocolate chips
1½ cups sweetened condensed milk
1 T. butter
2 tsp. vanilla
1 cup walnuts, optional

Make Dough: Cream together the butter and sugar. Add the eggs and beat well. Mix together the salt, baking soda, rolled oats, and flour and then gradually add to the creamed mixture, beating well after each addition.

Make Filling: In a medium saucepan, mix together filling ingredients except for walnuts. Over medium-low heat and stirring often, cook until chocolate is completely melted. Add walnuts if using and stir to mix; set aside.

In an ungreased 10 x 15 x 1-inch baking pan (or you can use a 9 x 13-inch pan, but you may need to bake the revel bars for 1-3 minutes longer) spread about ⅔ of the dough evenly across the bottom. Using a rubber spatula, scrape the filling onto the dough in the pan, spreading evenly. Dot the top with the remaining dough.

Bake at 350° for about 25 minutes or until top is golden. Cool so the chocolate sets up before cutting.

Notes:

76 Chocolate Peppermint Candy Cake

⅔ cup butter, room temperature
1⅔ cups granulated sugar
3 eggs
2 cups flour
⅔ cup cocoa powder
1¼ tsp. baking soda
¼ tsp. baking powder
1 tsp. salt
1⅓ cups milk
½ cup crushed peppermint candy canes (or other hard
    peppermint candy)

Chocolate Peppermint Frosting
½ cup butter
½ cup cocoa powder
3⅔ cups powdered sugar
7 T. milk
1 tsp. vanilla
1 T. crushed candy canes

Grease and flour two cake pans; set aside for now.

For the cake: In a large mixing bowl, cream together the butter, sugar, and eggs until well mixed and smooth; then beat on high speed for 3 minutes more.

Mix together the flour, cocoa powder, baking soda, baking powder, and salt; add to creamed mixture alternately with the milk, blending well after each addition. Blend in the crushed candy canes.

Spread batter evenly between the two cake pans and bake in a pre-heated 350° oven for 35 minutes. Cool for 10 minutes before slipping

Notes:

cakes from pan and allow them to cool completely before frosting them with chocolate peppermint frosting.

For the frosting: In a medium saucepan, melt the butter; stirring constantly. Add the cocoa powder and cook for about 1 minute until smooth; remove from heat. Beat in the powdered sugar and milk and continue beating (I do this by hand with a large wooden spoon or rotary egg beater) until mixture is smooth and of spreading consistency; add the vanilla and crushed candy canes and beat again until smooth. Spread between the layers and all around the top and sides of Chocolate Peppermint Candy Cake.

We love this cake and I always make it with candy canes, which means we have to wait for the holidays to make (and eat!) it. But it's worth the wait. The candy caramelizes on the bottom and the crunchy, minty taste is delightful!

Notes:

77 Cottage Pie

2 cups leftover cooked meat, diced (chicken, pork, beef, or
  hamburger, etc.)
2 T. butter
3 T. flour
1 can vegetable soup plus enough water to make a total of 2 cups
leftover mashed potatoes (or make a fresh batch, enough to
  cover your pie)

In a medium saucepan, melt the butter and add the diced meat; cook,
stirring, until meat is hot. Add the flour and stir until well blended.
Pour in the soup mixture and cook, stirring constantly, until the mixture has thickened.

Turn into a 9 x 9-inch baking dish and top with a thick layer of
mashed potatoes. Bake at 375° for about 20 minutes or until potatoes are lightly browned on top.

I often make this dish using hamburger that I cook fresh, and instead
of draining off the fat, I use that in place of some of the butter that's
needed to make the gravy. It gives a nice flavor to the finished dish.
And I usually use a quart jar of my home-canned vegetable soup in
place of the store-bought can of soup. Really, this is the sort of recipe
that doesn't take careful measuring. Just throw into the pot what you
have on hand and top with mashed potatoes that have been made
with rich milk and plenty of butter.

QUICK AND EASY DINNERS

Notes:

78 Creamy Potato Casserole

1 32-oz. package hash browns
1½ cups sour cream
¾ cup melted butter, divided
1½ cups shredded cheddar cheese
½ cup onion, finely diced
1 can cream of mushroom soup
salt and pepper to taste
2 cups crushed cornflakes

Mix together hash browns, sour cream, ½ cup melted butter, cheese, onion, soup, salt, and pepper. Pour into a 9 x 13-inch baking dish that has been lightly greased. (You can use cooking spray or butter.) Mix together ¼ cup of the melted butter and the cornflakes and sprinkle over the top.

Bake at 350° for 1 hour.

Notes:

79 Farmer's Soup

1 lb. hamburger
1 large onion, chopped
1 cup celery, chopped
1 large potato, peeled and diced (at least 1 cup)
1 cup carrots, peeled and sliced
salt and pepper to taste
1 cup tomato sauce
2½ quarts water
¼ cup cornmeal
¼ cup water

Brown the hamburger and onion and drain off fat. In a Dutch oven or heavy soup pot, add the meat and onion mixture, celery, potatoes, carrots, salt and pepper, tomato sauce, and 2½ quarts water. Simmer, covered, until vegetables are tender.

Just before serving, make a thin paste of the cornmeal and ¼ cup water. Add to the soup, stirring as you pour it in so it doesn't lump up. Continue stirring the soup until slightly thickened, about 2 minutes.

QUICK AND EASY DINNERS

Notes:

80 Gingerbread

½ cup boiling water
½ cup butter or shortening
½ cup brown sugar
¼ cup honey
½ cup molasses
1 egg, well beaten
1½ cups flour
½ tsp. salt
½ tsp baking powder
½ tsp. baking soda
¾ tsp. ginger
¾ tsp. cinnamon
¼ tsp. allspice

Pour boiling water over the butter; add the brown sugar, honey, molasses, and egg and beat well.

Sift together the dry ingredients; gradually add to the molasses mixture and beat until the batter is smooth.

Grease an 8-inch square pan and pour the batter into the pan; bake at 350° for 25 minutes or until done.

This is great served plain, but it's even better when served slightly warm with whipped cream on top.

Notes:

81 Ham Loaf

3 T. butter
5 T. brown sugar
3 slices pineapple
1½ lbs. cooked ground ham
½ cup breadcrumbs
¼ cup milk
2 eggs, slightly beaten
salt and pepper to taste

In the loaf pan you plan to use, melt the butter; add the brown sugar and stir until the sugar is dissolved. Lay in the pineapple slices evenly across the bottom of the pan.

Using your hands, mix together the ham, breadcrumbs, milk, eggs, and salt and pepper. Spread over the pineapple slices and bake at 375° for 1 hour. Turn out ham loaf on a serving platter so the pineapple is right-side-up and serve.

You might wonder where to get cooked ground ham, but there's an easy way to accomplish this at home if you don't have a meat grinder. You can easily find 1-lb. cans of cooked ham; buy two and either lavishly use it all in this recipe (if your loaf pan is big enough), or save out half of one can for something else such as scrambled eggs and diced ham for breakfast. Now all you need to do is smash the ham with a meat tenderizer or your hands. Voilà! Ground cooked ham ready to go.

Notes:

82 Hamburger Dressing Casserole

1 lb. hamburger
1 medium onion, chopped
1 can cream of chicken soup
1 can cream of celery or cream of mushroom soup
2 soup cans water or chicken broth
5 cups seasoned bread cubes or croutons
    (the kind you use in your turkey dressing)

In a large pot, brown hamburger and onion; drain off fat. Add the soups and water and mix.

Butter a large baking dish and spread the bread cubes evenly. Pour the soup and meat mixture evenly over the top of the bread cubes, adding a bit more water if you like your dressing moist.

Bake at 350° for 25 minutes or until bubbly and lightly browned on top.

Notes:

83 Haystack Supper

This recipe makes enough for 2 casseroles, so you will be dividing the ingredients into 2 baking dishes.

40 saltine or Ritz crackers, crushed
2 cups cooked rice
3 lb. hamburger
1 large onion, chopped
1½ cups tomato juice or sauce
¾ cup water
3 T. taco seasoning
salt and pepper to taste
4 cups lettuce, shredded
3 medium tomatoes, diced
½ cup butter, cubed
½ cup flour
4 cups milk
1 lb. Velveeta cheese, cubed
3 cups sharp cheddar cheese, shredded
1 can pitted olives
1 package (about 14½ oz.) tortilla chips

Divide crackers between two ungreased 10 x 9-inch baking pans. Top each with rice, spread evenly over the crackers.

In a large skillet, brown the hamburger and onion; drain. Add the tomato juice, water, and seasonings and simmer for 20 minutes. Spoon meat mixture over rice. Next, layer on the lettuce and tomatoes.

In a large saucepan, melt the butter. Stir in the flour and continue stirring until mixture is smooth. Gradually add the milk. Continue stirring, bring to a boil, and cook until the sauce thickens, about 2

Notes:

minutes. Reduce heat to low and stir in Velveeta cheese until melted. Pour cheese mixture over the lettuce and tomatoes.

Top with Cheddar cheese and olives and serve with the tortilla chips.

Haystack Supper is a very forgiving meal. You can add or omit ingredients depending on what you have on hand or what your family is especially fond of. You can also put the individual ingredients into serving dishes and everyone can concoct their own haystack at the table. It's fun!

84 Layered Lettuce and Pea Salad

1 head iceberg lettuce, coarsely shredded or chopped
½ cup sliced celery
¼ cup diced onion
½ cup chopped green peppers
1 10-oz. package frozen peas, or about 2 cups
2 cups mayonnaise
½ cup grated Cheddar cheese
6 slices bacon, cooked and chopped, or about ½ cup bacon bits,
  more or less

In a casserole dish or large salad bowl, layer the first 6 ingredients in the order given. Cover and refrigerate for at least 6 hours. When ready to serve, sprinkle on the cheese and bacon bits.

Sometimes I make this salad with fresh peas instead of frozen, which I personally like better.

QUICK AND EASY DINNERS

Notes:

85 Leftover Meat Pie

double crust pie shell, unbaked
1½ cups leftover meat, more or less, cut in small cubes
½ cup vegetables, more or less, cooked and diced, such as
    potatoes, carrots, corn, onions, or peas
¼ cup drippings or broth, or 1 cup gravy and omit the milk
    (below)
3 T. flour
1 cup milk
salt and pepper to taste

Heat drippings; gradually add flour, stirring constantly. Once the roux is smooth, gradually add milk and continue to cook, stirring constantly, until sauce thickens. (If you have leftover gravy, you can skip this step and simply heat the gravy in a saucepan.)

Mix the meat and vegetables into the gravy and pour into an unbaked pie crust. Place the top crust on, crimp the edges, and make several small slashes across the top to vent.

Bake at 425° for 25 minutes or until the crust is golden and the meat filling is bubbling.

This is a forgiving recipe. You can use nothing but meat if that's all you have. Mix and match vegetables to suit your taste. Also, once you add the meat, try not to overstir—stirring too much will shred the meat.

Notes:

86 Pistachio Delight

First Layer
1 cup walnuts, finely chopped
2 cups flour
1 cup butter, room temperature

Second Layer
4 oz. cream cheese
1 cup powdered sugar
1 cup sweetened whipped cream or Cool Whip

Third Layer
2 3½-oz boxes instant pistachio pudding
2¾ cups cold milk
1 tsp. vanilla

First layer: Mix together all ingredients and press into a 9 x 13-inch baking pan. Bake at 350° for 15 minutes; cool completely.

Second layer: Cream together the cream cheese and powdered sugar until smooth. Fold in whipped cream, blending well. Spread evenly over cooled crust.

Third layer: Mix together all ingredients and beat for 2 minutes. Spread over the top of the cream cheese mixture. Refrigerate. When ready to serve, you can add more sweetened whipped cream and sprinkle on some chopped nuts if desired.

Notes:

87 Poor Man's Steak

1 lb. hamburger
1 cup cracker crumbs
1 cup milk
1 tsp. salt
¼ tsp. pepper
1 small onion, chopped (optional)
1 can cream of mushroom soup
½ soup can water

Mix together all ingredients except the soup and water. Press into a cookie sheet or loaf pan and refrigerate at least 8 hours or overnight.

When ready to bake, cut the meat into slices or rectangles about 3 x 4 inches. Dredge in flour and brown in a lightly oiled frying pan so they don't stick.

Lay the pieces in a roasting pan close together in one layer. Mix together the soup and water and spread over the meat. Bake at 350° for 1 hour.

Notes:

88 Potato Chip Chicken Casserole

3 cups chicken, cooked and cubed
3 cups crushed potato chips (there can still be small pieces)
1 can cream of mushroom or cream of chicken soup
1 soup can milk
½ cup mayonnaise
2 ribs celery, diced
½ cup almonds, optional
¾ cup cheddar cheese, optional

Mix together the soup, milk, mayonnaise, celery, and almonds (if using).

In a greased or buttered 10 x 13-inch baking dish, make two layers in the order given: half the chicken, a third of the potato chips, and a third of the soup mixture. Repeat these layers and end with the last third of the soup mixture followed by the last third of the potato chips. Top with shredded cheddar cheese if desired.

Bake at 350° for about 40-45 minutes.

Notes:

89 Potato Rivvel Soup

3 lbs. potatoes, peeled and cubed
½ cup onion, diced
pinch of salt
2 T. butter
salt and pepper to taste
1 cup milk, more or less
1 cup water, more or less

Rivvels
1 cup flour
½ tsp. salt
1 egg, beaten

Put potatoes and onion in a large kettle with water to barely cover and a pinch of salt and cook until the potatoes are done; do not drain. Take a potato masher and mash the potatoes in the water until they are roughly mashed. There will still be small lumps. Then add the butter and salt and pepper to taste.

Next add the milk and water—you need to use a combination of milk and water because the milk gives the soup a creamy richness and the water thins it enough to be called "soup." Bring the soup to a gentle bubbling simmer.

Make the *rivvels:* In a medium bowl, mix the flour and salt. Make a well in the middle and then pour the egg into the well. Mix together until you have lumps of dough about the size of peas or small grapes. This is a fairly messy process, so feel free to use your hands to mix. Drop these *rivvels* into the simmering soup and, stirring occasionally, cook them until done, about 10 minutes or so depending on their size. If the soup is too thick, you can add more milk. Adjust the seasoning to taste before serving.

Notes:

QUICK AND EASY DINNERS

Potato Rivvel Soup is a favorite during winter. It sticks to your ribs, is inexpensive to make, and kids love it. If you have anyone who is averse to onions, you can always omit them and simply add some onion powder instead. Then everyone is happy!

Once you get the hang of it, you can use any amount of potatoes—just add more milk, water, and butter to compensate. When I make a big batch I will often double the *rivvels* recipe, using 2 eggs, ¾ tsp. salt, and about 1¾ cups flour. And if company is coming, I throw in a few pinches of parsley for looks. But really, any way you make this, it's just plain great eating.

90 Rivvel Soup

1 quart chicken broth
1 cup corn, frozen, canned and drained, or fresh off the cob
1 cup flour
½ tsp. salt
1 egg, beaten

In a medium saucepan bring the chicken broth to a boil.

Meanwhile, mix together the flour and salt. Make a well in the middle and add the beaten egg. First with a fork, and then using your fingers, mix the flour and egg together until you have lumps about the size of grapes.

Add the *rivvels* to the broth, stirring while you pour them in. Next, add the corn and cook, stirring occasionally, for about 10 minutes or until *rivvels* are done. The time will vary somewhat depending on how big your *rivvels* are. If the soup is too thick, you can add more broth or some milk and heat through before serving.

Notes:

91 Scalloped Corn Casserole

1 quart corn (canned and drained, frozen corn that has been
    thawed, or fresh cooked)
1 cup cracker or bread crumbs
2 eggs
½ cup milk
salt and pepper to taste

Place the corn and crumbs in layers in a buttered casserole dish, keeping out a bit of crumbs to sprinkle on top.

In a small mixing bowl, beat the eggs well; add the milk, salt, and pepper. Carefully pour over the corn and crumbs; top with the remaining crumbs and bake at 350° for 20 minutes or until bubbly and golden on top.

QUICK AND EASY DINNERS

Notes:

92 Scalloped Potatoes

6 large russet potatoes, peeled and thinly sliced
9 T. flour
6 T. cold butter, finely cubed
1 quart milk (more or less)
salt and pepper to taste
¾ cup Cheddar cheese, optional

Butter a 9 x 13-inch baking dish. Add a third of the potatoes and sprinkle with a third (3 T.) of the flour and a third (2 T.) of the butter; repeat layers two more times. Carefully pour in the milk until it covers about ¾ of the potatoes.

Bake in a preheated 425° oven for 15 minutes; reduce heat to 375° and continue baking until done, about another 45-60 minutes. If desired, during the last 15 minutes, sprinkle on Cheddar cheese and finish baking.

Notes:

93 Stewed Tomatoes and Dumplings

Stewed Tomatoes
¼ cup butter
½ cup onion, chopped
¼ cup celery, chopped
2 quarts home-canned tomatoes or 1 28-oz. can whole tomatoes,
    coarsely chopped with juice
2 tsp. brown sugar
½ tsp. salt
½ tsp. dried basil
½ tsp. pepper

Dumplings
1 cup flour
1½ tsp. baking powder
½ tsp. salt
1 T. butter
1 egg, beaten
6 T. milk
1 T. fresh parsley, minced or 1 heaping tsp. dried

QUICK AND EASY DINNERS

In a medium-large saucepan, melt the butter and sauté the onion and celery about 3 minutes. Add the tomatoes and juice, brown sugar, and seasonings and bring to a boil. Simmer uncovered for several minutes.

In a medium mixing bowl, combine the flour, baking powder, and salt for the dumplings. Cut in the butter using a pastry blender or two knives until the mixture resembles coarse cornmeal. Add the egg, milk, and parsley and blend lightly. Do not overmix. Drop dumplings by tablespoonfuls on top of the simmering tomato mixture. Cover pot tightly and cook over medium-low heat for 20 minutes. (Don't lift the lid during this cooking period.) Serve in bowls, topped with a pat of butter if desired.

Notes:

94 Stonaflesch

2 lb. hamburger
10 carrots, peeled and sliced
6 large potatoes, peeled and thinly sliced
salt and pepper
paprika
thyme, optional

In a heavy ovenproof pot, layer a portion of the raw hamburger with some of the carrots and then potatoes. When each layer has been completed, salt and pepper (also adding a sprinkle of thyme if desired) and then continue layering. It's better to have several thin layers rather than just a few thick ones. Be sure to end with a small amount of hamburger. Sprinkle paprika over the top and cover with a tight-fitting lid.

Bake at 350° for at least an hour, or until carrots and potatoes are cooked through and tender. If you have the time, bake it at 250° for 3-4 hours, being careful not to scorch the bottom.

You can also cook this all day on low in a slow cooker, but add about 2 T. water or broth to the pot.

Notes:

95 Strawberry Pretzel Salad

1 cup pretzels, coarsely crushed
½ cup sugar
¾ cup butter, softened
⅓ cup chopped nuts
1 8-oz. package cream cheese
1 cup sugar
1 cup whipping cream, whipped
1 6-oz. box strawberry Jell-O
2 cups boiling water
2 10-oz. boxes frozen strawberries
   (or use 2½–3 cups fresh sliced strawberries)

Mix together the crushed pretzels, ½ cup sugar, butter, and nuts. Press the mixture lightly into a greased rectangular glass baking dish. Bake 10 minutes in a 350° oven. Cool.

Combine the cream cheese, 1 cup sugar, and whipped cream. Spread on the cooled pretzel layer and refrigerate.

Dissolve the Jell-O in the boiling water. Add the frozen strawberries. When 75 percent set, put on top of the cream cheese layer. Refrigerate for several hours or overnight.

QUICK AND EASY DINNERS

Notes:

111

96 Sweet Potato Fries

4 sweet potatoes, skinned and sliced the long way
2-3 T. oil
1 tsp. salt
large pinch hot ground pepper, such as cayenne

Place the potato slices in a gallon freezer bag and drizzle the oil, salt, and pepper over them. Close up the bag and shake to coat the slices as evenly as possible.

Bake at 450° for about 20 minutes or until tender and lightly browned, turning once.

You can use this recipe with russet potatoes as well, but I usually leave out the hot pepper and instead add some non-salt seasoning or paprika. Also, we like our fries a bit on the crispy side so I tend to roast them a bit longer, depending on the thickness of the slices.

QUICK AND EASY DINNERS

Notes:

97 Vegetable Oyster Soup
(Poor Man's Oyster Stew)

1½ cups salsify root, peeled and diced
½ cup onions, carrots, and celery
    (choose how much of each you want), finely diced
2 cups water
1 T. vinegar
1 T. butter
1 quart milk or half-and-half
salt and pepper to taste

In a heavy saucepot, mix together the salsify, vegetables, water, and vinegar. Simmer until vegetables are tender; drain. Add butter, milk, and salt and pepper to taste; bring to a simmer and serve.

Salsify is a member of the dandelion family, but you use the root part of the plant, which is suggestive of a thin parsnip. The ugly looking "skin" of the salsify belies the delicately flavored root's interior. Some folks think salsify tastes a bit like oysters; thus the name "Poor Man's Oyster Stew."

QUICK AND EASY DINNERS

Notes:

98 **Whoopie Pies**

Cookies
2 cups flour
½ cup cocoa powder
1 tsp. baking soda
¼ tsp. salt
½ cup shortening
1 cup sugar
1 egg plus 1 egg yolk
1 tsp. vanilla
1 cup buttermilk
1 cup hot water

Filling
1½ cups marshmallow fluff or marshmallow crème
1¼ cups shortening
1 cup powdered sugar
1 T. vanilla

Preheat oven to 450°. Line cookie sheets with parchment paper or silicone sheets.

In a medium mixing bowl, combine the flour, cocoa powder, baking soda, and salt; set aside for now.

In a large mixing bowl, cream together ½ cup shortening and sugar until light and fluffy. Add the egg, egg yolk, and vanilla and beat for 2 minutes more. Add ⅓ of the flour mixture and beat on low speed just until combined. Add the buttermilk, ⅓ of the flour mixture, the hot water, and the remaining flour mixture, beating on low speed with each addition until combined.

Notes:

Drop the dough onto the prepared cookie sheets using about 2 tsp. for each cookie. Bake for about 5 minutes; let cool on the cookie sheets for several minutes and then remove them to a wire rack to cool completely.

In the meantime, make the filling. Cream together the marshmallow crème and shortening for about 3 minutes, using an electric beater and beating until the mixture is light and fluffy. Reduce speed to lowest setting and mix in the powdered sugar, a bit at a time; add the vanilla. Now increase the speed to medium and beat the filling until light and fluffy, about another 3 minutes.

To make the whoopie pies, spread some filling on the bottom side of half of the cookies and then place another cookie (top side out) on the filling. Press gently but not so hard that the filling oozes out.

Whoopie Pies store well for several days in an airtight container. (No need to refrigerate.)

Notes:

99 Yumasetta

2 lb. hamburger
salt and pepper to taste
2 T. brown sugar
½ cup onion, chopped
½ cup celery, chopped
1 can tomato soup
1 16-oz. package egg noodles
1 can cream of chicken soup
1 cup Velveeta cheese, sliced or cubed

Brown hamburger with salt, pepper, brown sugar, onion, and celery; drain off grease. Add tomato soup to the meat mixture and mix.

Meanwhile, cook the egg noodles according to package directions; drain. Stir in cream of chicken soup and mix.

In a 13 x 9-inch baking dish layer hamburger mixture and noodle mixture with Velveeta cheese between layers.

Bake at 350° for about 30 minutes or until the cheese is melted and casserole is bubbly.

Notes:

RECIPE INDEX

Best-Ever Breakfasts

Midday Meals and Snacks

Quick and Easy Dinners

The Homestyle Amish Kitchen Cookbook

Plainly Delicious Recipes from the Simple Life

Just about everyone is fascinated by the Amish—their simple, family-centered lifestyle, colorful quilts, and hearty, homemade meals. Straight from the heart of Amish country, this celebration of hearth and home will delight readers with the pleasures of the family table as they take a peek at the Amish way of life—a life filled with the self-reliance and peace of mind that many of us long for.

Readers will appreciate the scores of tasty, easy-to-prepare recipes such as Scrapple, Graham "Nuts" Cereal, Potato Rivvel Soup, Amish Dressing, and Snitz Pie. At the same time they'll learn a bit about the Amish, savor interesting tidbits from the "Amish Kitchen Wisdom" sections, find out just how much food it takes to feed the large number of folks attending preaching services, barn raisings, weddings, and work frolics, and much more.

The Homestyle Amish Kitchen Cookbook is filled with good, old-fashioned family meal ideas to help bring the simple life home!

The Amish Canning Cookbook

Plain and Simple Living at Its Homemade Best

From the author of *The Homestyle Amish Kitchen Cookbook* comes a great new collection of recipes, hints, and Plain wisdom for everyone who loves the idea of preserving fresh, wholesome foods. Whether instructing a beginning canner or helping a seasoned cook hone her skills, certified Master Food Preserver Georgia Varozza shows people how to get the very best out of their food. Here, readers will find...

- a short history of canning
- lists of all the tools and supplies needed to get started
- basic instructions for safe canning
- recipes for canning fruit, vegetables, meat, soups, sauces, and more
- guidelines for adapting recipes to fit personal tastes

With its expert advice and warm tones, *The Amish Canning Cookbook* will become a beloved companion to those who love the tradition, frugality, and homestyle flavor of Amish cooking!

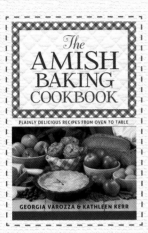

The Amish Baking Cookbook
Plainly Delicious Recipes from Oven to Table

Building on the success of *The Homestyle Amish Kitchen* (more than 60,000 copies sold), Georgia Varozza partners with experienced baker Kathleen Kerr to give you a cookbook filled with the foods most associated with the Plain and simple life: baked goods. This delicious collection of more than three hundred classic baking recipes for cookies, cakes, pies, bars, and breads inspires you who love Amish fiction and are drawn to the Plain lifestyle to roll up your sleeves and start baking!

Whether you consider yourself a novice or a veteran in the kitchen, Georgia and Kathleen make it easy to make delicious baking recipes such as Amish Nut Balls and Brown Sugar Pie. Find the perfect recipe to prepare for that large weekend potluck, tonight's intimate family dinner, or a fun activity with the kids.

What the Amish Can Teach Us About the Simple Life

Homespun Hints for Family Gatherings, Spending Less, and Sharing Your Bounty

Emphasizing Amish values of faith, simplicity, and self-sufficiency, author Georgia Varozza offers fresh ideas to make faith, serenity, and healthy living a stronger presence in everyday life. Drawing on her family's Plain roots, she provides innovative suggestions and easy-to-follow instructions to help readers

- create a home atmosphere that promotes faith and family
- simplify their lives by controlling technology
- enjoy the satisfaction of successful do-it-yourself projects
- discover the benefits of growing and raising their own food
- generate less waste by repurposing, reusing, and recycling

Practical and hands-on, this book is a great resource for people who want to make a few simple changes or fully embrace a more wholesome lifestyle.

501 Time-Saving Tips Every Woman Should Know
Get More Done in Less Time with Less Stress

Would you like some help with your to-do list? Who wouldn't! You'll love these surprisingly quick, easy, and effective ways to complete troublesome tasks in a snap.

- A squeegee or dryer sheet works great for removing pet hair from your furniture and carpet.

- Plain, whole-milk yogurt and a cold-water rinse soothe sunburned skin.

- Add Epsom salts to your watering can to make your garden more productive.

- Put baking soda and vinegar to work removing spots from your old baking pans.

- Use ice cubes to restore your carpet where furniture has left indentations.

You don't have to work harder. Just get smarter—and enjoy the time you'll save.

To learn more about Harvest House books and
to read sample chapters, visit our website:

www.harvesthousepublishers.com

HARVEST HOUSE PUBLISHERS
EUGENE, OREGON